36th Congress, 2d Session. } HOUSE OF REPRESENTATIVES.

RELATIVE TO THE CORRESPONDENCE BETWEEN THE PRESIDENT AND THE COMMISSIONERS ON THE PART OF THE STATE OF SOUTH CAROLINA.

February 27, 1861.—Ordered to be printed, together with the views of the minority, and recommitted to the select committee.

Mr. Reynolds, from the select committee, made the following

REPORT:

The select committee to whom was referred the message of the President of the United States, bearing date the 8th day of January, 1861, *with special instructions, submit, in partial discharge of the duties imposed upon them, the following report:*

Accompanying the message of the President, referred to this committee, is a copy of certain correspondence had between the President and Messrs. R. W. Barnwell, J. H. Adams, and James L. Orr, claiming to be "commissioners" on the part of the State of South Carolina, "authorized and empowered to treat with the government of the United States for the delivery of the forts, magazines, light-houses, and other real estate, with their appurtenances, within the limits of South Carolina, and also for the apportionment of the public debt, and a division of all other property held by the government of the United States as agent of the confederated States, of which South Carolina was recently a member, and generally to negotiate as to all other measures and arrangements proper to be made and adopted in the existing relations of the parties, and for the continuance of peace and amity between the commonwealth (South Carolina) and the government at Washington."

A further message of the President, under date of February 8, 1861, and referred to this committee, communicates a copy of certain correspondence growing out of another special mission from the State of South Carolina to the President of the United States, having for its object a demand upon the government of the United States for "the delivery of Fort Sumter, in the harbor of Charleston, to the constituted authorities of the State of South Carolina."

The correspondence above referred to is submitted by the President without comment or any suggestion as to the propriety or necessity of any action by Congress in respect to it or to the various subjects to which it refers. If important to be submitted to Congress at all, it seems certainly to be of a character demanding grave consideration; and the fact that it has been placed before us by the President implies that, in his opinion, at least, it involved considerations which might properly engage the attention of the legislative branch of the government in connexion with the various other matters forced upon it by the necessities of the times. The committee has therefore thought it expedient and proper to direct attention to these special embassies, their object, the action of the President thereon, and incidentally to the character of the correspondence.

The first communication to the President, by Messrs. Barnwell, Adams, and Orr, under date of December 28, 1860, communicates an official copy of an ordinance of secession, adopted by the State of South Carolina on the 20th of the same month, by virtue of which that State assumes to have withdrawn from the federal Union, and taken the position of an entirely independent nation. That such an attitude was assumed by South Carolina in attempting negotiations with the government of the United States is not only obvious from the history of current events, but it was most distinctly asserted by her "commissioners" in their communication to the President. The movement of Major Anderson from Fort Moultrie to Fort Sumter, after their arrival in Washington, seems to have been regarded as an obstacle on their part to the opening of any discussion touching the object of their mission until the circumstances attending that movement should be explained in a manner which should relieve them of all doubt as to the spirit in which the contemplated negotiations should be conducted. They, however, urge upon the President the immediate withdrawal of the troops of the United States from the harbor of Charleston, upon the allegation that they are a standing menace, which rendered negotiations impossible, and which, as they express it, "threatens speedily to bring to a bloody issue questions which ought to be settled with temperance and judgment." This communication was received by the President, and made the subject of a formal and elaborate reply. Considering the position assumed by the President in his annual message in respect to the right of a State to withdraw from the Union, and the total absence of power on the part of the Executive to recognize the validity of any such attempt, the committee cannot but regard the mission itself, as well as the manner in which it has been treated by the President, as among the most remarkable events of the extraordinary times in which we live. In his annual message, communicated to Congress at the beginning of the present session, the position is most distinctly affirmed by the President that no State has the constitutional right to withdraw from the Union, and that there is no power in the executive department of the government to give the slightest countenance or encouragement to any such attempt. In this opinion we fully concur; and, believing it to be the true theory of the Constitution, we have been unable to perceive upon what principle the President, representing the dignity of the government of the United States, has assumed to entertain or hold any official communication of the character disclosed with the representatives of the State of South Carolina. For it seems to us obvious enough that, upon the principles enunciated in the annual message, the gentlemen composing this commission, acting under the sanction of a disloyal State, could be regarded in no other light than as engaged in a revolutionary effort to subvert the government of the United States; and being so regarded, it would appear to have been the plain duty of the Executive to enforce the laws against any individuals, however eminent and respectable, known or suspected of complicity in any movement of a treasonable character. We are not able to imagine any circumstances under which the President of the United States would be justified in entertaining diplomatic intercourse with the State of South Carolina in her present attitude to the general government, except upon the assumption that, by the action of her authorities, she had succeeded in acquiring the position of an independent power, owing no duty whatever to the government of the United States.

As before stated, it is claimed by her, and on her behalf, that she now occupies such a position, and her agents are sent hither upon that assumption, charged with most extraordinary and insolent demands upon the President. The reception by the President of such a communication, under such circumstances, and awarding the dignity of an official reply, involves, to some extent, a recognition of the assumed position of the rebellious State, and impliedly admits that the individuals engaged in the revolutionary movements against the federal government have acquired a political position which entitles them to some other consideration than is most commonly due to those who invite a collision with established authority. It is this attitude of the President's that the committee particularly desire to express dissent from, and to affirm, most emphatically, the doctrine that so long as the federal government exists its Constitution and laws operate with full vigor upon the people of every State, and that no action of State authority, of less degree than successful revolution, can justify any department of the government in treating any persons engaged in the effort to throw of all federal obligations other than as rebels and traitors, and entitled to be dealt with as such.

Even if, from any considerations growing out of the structure of our government, or the dangerous tendency of the secession movement in several States of the Union—the anxiety to prevent the shedding of blood and of avoiding the evils of civil war—great forbearance in the actual enforcement of the laws against political offenders may be pardoned and perhaps justified, we are not prepared to give our assent to any action of the executive department which in express terms, or by a necessary implication, may seem to place the responsible actors and abettors of secession in any State of the Union in any other aspect than that of traitors to the Constitution of the United States.

It is believed that the assertion and maintenance of this position is essential to the existence of the federal government, and without which it neither can have nor deserve obedience at home or respect abroad. It may, perhaps, for a time, be tolerated that offenders against the laws may be permitted to go "unwhipped of justice." The forcible seizure of public property by rebellious citizens may temporarily be allowed to pass unpunished, for reasons which may appear satisfactory to those charged with executive duty, but this condition of things cannot be of long continuance. Either the government must vindicate its power, or it will itself become powerless. If any portion of the people of the republic may at their pleasure repudiate all federal authority, defy and disorganize the government, seize its property and insult its flag, without incurring the hazard of punishment for treason, either by civil or military authority, we may well admit there is no government of the United States worthy of preservation.

And if, after the people of a State, without adequate cause, have announced their purpose of repudiating all allegiance to the federal Union, they are, without question, to be entertained by the government of the United States with diplomatic intercourse in respect to the abandonment of its own forts, arsenals, and other public buildings, upon threats of forcible expulsion if the demands upon it are not at once acceded to, we may well pause and consider to what depths of degradation and humiliation the American government is approaching, if the lowest depth has not already been reached.

The committee do not propose to discuss here whether it is wise or politic, at the present time, to employ the whole power of the government, under all circumstances, and at all hazards, to punish offenders against its laws. In times of extensive civil commotion and discontent, prudence may dictate great caution and forbearance in the exercise of acknowledged powers; and when whole communities assume the attitude of revolution against established government for real or imaginary wrongs, it may be wise to listen to their complaints with attention, and not, by any unnecessary rigor against palpable violations of law, provoke passions already unduly and unreasonably excited.

But when growing discontent assumes the position of actual hostility; when, instead of seeking redress under existing forms, resort is had to force, and the purpose is boldly avowed of overturning the government to which their allegiance is due, we cannot see the wisdom of a policy which permits treason to perform its work without hindrance or molestation. Above all, we cannot sanction a policy in the executive department of this government which professes a purpose of executing its laws and protecting its property from unlawful violence, and yet remains inactive when revolution is actually impending, and entertains friendly intercourse with embassies instigated by and growing out of the highest type of treason to the federal Constitution.

The President acknowledges the obligations of his oath to protect and defend the Constitution, and enforce the laws made in obedience to its requirements; denies the right of secession; and yet, in the correspondence before us, we have the evidence that, with full knowledge that the authority of the government has been set at defiance, its dignity insulted, and its flag dishonored, he yet negotiates with treason, and commits the government to a partial recognition of the revolutionary movement for its destruction. If, for any considerations of policy, he may be justified in suspending the exercise of its powers, we know of no reason that can justify a course of action which ignores the theory upon which the whole foundation of the government rests. If the fact that the government has the power to protect itself from domestic violence may not prudently be acted upon, under an apprehension that any exercise of authority may irritate and exasperate those already in open rebellion, it would be some consolation to such of the citizens of the United States as are still loyal to the Constitution to feel assured that the desire to shield traitors from the consequences of their acts may not result in the utter demoralization of all federal authority and dignity.

If we recur to the contents of the correspondence to which we have referred, there is but little to commend it to favorable consideration. The communication by the "commissioners" of South Carolina to the President conveys, in the most unqualified terms, an imputation of bad faith upon the President, and, of necessity, upon the government of the United States, on account of the occupation of Fort Sumter by Major Anderson and his command. It is clearly intimated that some agreement, previously made by the President, respecting the occupation of the forts in the harbor of Charleston, had been violated. From this charge the President has undertaken to defend himself, and to furnish excuses for the action of the government in respect to the occupation of its own fortresses and the disposition of its own troops. The fact that the State of South Carolina intended to rebel against the government of the United States was well understood long before her ordinance of secession was actually adopted. The probable consequences of such action, it was also well known, would be an attempt on the part of the State to take possession of all the forts, arsenals, magazines, and other public property within her limits. Under such circumstances, nothing would seem to be clearer than the duty of the President to provide in due time an adequate force for the protection of all the public property in danger of assault. Instead, however, of taking such a course, the President seems to have been in communication with those engaged in the rebellion; and a sort of understanding appears to have been had early in December that no action should be taken by the government of the United States to reinforce the command charged with the defence of the forts in the harbor of Charleston.

On the 9th of December, 1860, the representatives in Congress from the State of South Carolina furnished the President with a written statement, under their signatures, expressing their strong conviction that the forts in the harbor of Charleston would not be attacked or molested *previously* to the action of the convention of that State then about to assemble, and they hoped and believed not until after an offer had been made, through an accredited representative, to negotiate for an amicable arrangement of all matters between the State and the federal government, "*provided*, that no re-enforcements shall be sent into those forts, and their relative military status shall remain as at present."

At the time this paper was presented the President objected to the word "*provided*," as it might, as he expressed it, be construed into an agreement on his part which he "never would make." It was, he thinks, obvious there could be no such *agreement* made, and he says it was regarded, in effect, as the promise of highly honorable gentlemen to exert their influence for the purpose expressed. The purpose of the President was well known not to re-enforce the forts in Charleston harbor until they had been actually attacked, or until he had certain evidence that they were about to be attacked; and we are informed by his communication before us that, in respect to these forts, he acted in the same manner that he would have done if he had entered into a formal agreement with parties capable of contracting. It does not, therefore, appear to be material whether, in a strict technical sense, there was or was not an agreement to the effect indicated in the paper lodged with him by the representatives in Congress from the State of South Carolina. It is perfectly clear that at that time it was regarded as certain that South Carolina would attempt to secede from the Union, and intended to obtain possession of these forts, either by force or negotiation. With a knowledge of these purposes, the President is determined to send the officer in command no re-enforcements, and he has acted in this respect in the same manner as he would have done if he had made a formal agreement to that effect.

In this disclosure the committee are not able to resist the inference that in the beginning of the revolutionary movement against the government of the United States there were relations of an extremely friendly character between those who contemplated rebellion and those whose duty it was to suppress it. We cannot but regard it as a most extraordinary fact that parties notoriously contemplating the disruption of the government should beforehand stipulate with its executive authority in respect to the most convenient and least dangerous mode for making the rebellion successful. While the President has avowed his determination to execute the laws, he does not seem to have regarded treason to the Constitution of the United States, contemplated and existing, as among the crimes condemned by the laws of the land and deserving punishment.

That crime, the highest known to the laws of the world, appears in our history to have assumed a milder form, to be treated with marked tenderness by the authorities of the government against which the crime is perpetrated. We do not think the history of any government furnishes in this respect any parallel to the policy of our own; and we cannot believe that any government, however powerful, can long survive the inauguration of and persistence in such a policy. We therefore regard it our duty to condemn, in the most emphatic terms, the course pursued by the President in recognizing or substantially holding diplomatic communication with the rebellious authorities of the State of South Carolina. The dignity of the government required at least that the President should at once, and with firmness, decline all negotiations with a State in the attitude of rebellion, if the obligations of his oath did not require him to hand over such of the rebels as came within his power to the civil authorities of the United States, to be dealt with according to the forms of law.

Even while these negotiations were going on the President received information that the authorities of the State of South Carolina had seized by force Castle Pinckney, Fort Moultrie, the United States arsenal, aud the custom-house and post office in the city of Charleston. Although the correspondence before us does not disclose the facts, the history of the times furnishes us with the results of this "peace policy." In several other States of the Union the authority of the government of the United States has been defied and insulted, its flag dishonored, and its property unlawfully seized. No effort has been made to defend or recover it; and now a revolutionary government, embracing six of the States of the Union, (in all of which acts of violence against the property of the United States have been committed,) is set up in defiance of and in hostility to the government of the United States.

This revolutionary government must either be recognized or repudiated. Its independence must be acknowledged, or the persons engaged in the effort to establish it must be treated as rebels and traitors to the Constitution of the United States. To acknowledge the right of secession, or recognize the revolutionary acts growing out of it, is a surrender of the authority, power, and dignity of the government of the United States, and a substantial agreement to its destruction. We cannot believe that the American people will consent to the dissolution of the federal Union without an effort to save it, even if that effort involves a resort to all the powers which the government is able to command. That it can be preserved by peaceful negotiation and compromise does not seem probable, for in certain quarters all propositions of that character are most distinctly repudiated. The demand is made that the government of the United States shall surrender its authority, or maintain it by force of arms. We can imagine but one answer that ought to be given to such a demand, and the longer it is delayed the more disastrous may be the consequences to those who resist, as well as to those who desire to maintain, the integrity, the dignity, and the authority of the most beneficent government established since the foundation of the world.

The correspondence growing out of the mission of Colonel Hayne, "special envoy" from the State of South Carolina, communicated with the message of the 8th of February, 1861, is also before us. The object of the mission, as already stated, was to demand of the President the unconditional surrender of Fort Sumter to the authorities of the State of South Carolina, accompanied with a threat that if the demand was refused it would be taken by force of arms. The views we express as to the duty of the President in relation to the first mission apply with equal, if not greater force, to that represented by Colonel Hayne, as special envoy. If it were possible, the character of the second mission is even more insulting and offensive to the government of the United States than the first. In both instances, the President refused to accede to the demands made upon him; but, in our judgment, this fact does not remove the objections urged against the propriety of receiving or entertaining communications with any "commissioners" or "envoys" from States in the condition of actual rebellion against the government, who come, not to obtain pardon for their offences, but with demands which cannot, without disgrace and humiliation, be for one moment entertained.

Whatever consequences may follow the effort to maintain the dignity and integrity of the government of the United States, it seems impossible to contemplate the possibility of its peaceful destruction. So long as it has the power of self-preservation, there appears to be no alternative between its exercise, at whatever hazard, and a cowardly surrender, without a blow struck, upon the demand of rebels and traitors.

Your committee insist upon maintaining the dignity and exercising the powers of the government against any who deliberately set about its destruction, or invite collision with its power or its laws.

In conclusion, the committee recommend the adoption of the following resolution:

Resolved, That in the opinion of this House the President had no constitutional power to negotiate with the representatives of the State of South Carolina for the surrender of any public property within the limits of that State, and that it is inexpedient for Congress to take any further action in relation thereto.

MINORITY REPORT.

Mr. John Cochrane, from the committee of five, to whom was referred the President's communication of the 8th ultimo, with certain instructions, and his subsequent communication of the 9th instant, presents, by leave of the House, the following minority report, upon so much of the said reference as relates to the correspondence between the President and those invested by the State of South Carolina with diplomatic character.

A recurrence to events will enable the judgment to pronounce with more certainty and justice upon the acts of the President, which seem to have irritated the patriotism and provoked the animadversion of the majority of the committee. Their startling array marshals to us a connexion of facts unparalleld, if not hitherto supposed to be without the pale of political possibility. The sovereign State of South Carolina, for causes of assumed adequacy, severed the federation bonds which embraced her, and, by inherent sovereignty, constituted herself an independent State. Were we to receive her declarations as political doctrine, and her public acts as infrangible authority, she thereby emerged from the thraldom of the confederate Union, and maintained, what she assumed, the attitude and power of a rightful independence. In pursuance of her designs, the regenerated State authenticated commissioners to treat with the President of the United States concerning mutual rights, in abeyance between them. Among those enumerated appear to have been the fortifications, arsenals, magazines, light-houses, &c., the real property of the United States, and its appurtenances, together with the values they represented. The advent of the commissioners was recognized by the President as the arrival in Washington of distinguished citizens. Their interviews with him partook of the private consideration in which they were held; and the routine of colloquial interviews might have illimitably continued, had they not been terminated by the startling intelligence, that Major Anderson, in his literal compliance with the instructions of the President, had made more secure the property of the United States in Charleston harbor, concerning which it was the intent of the commissioners to treat. This event was the signal for the first written communication from the commissioners to the President, in which they displayed a copy of their instructions and powers. The President in reply uses the following language:

"In answer to this communication I have to say, that my position as President of the United States was clearly defined in the message to Congress on the 3d instant. In that I stated that 'apart from the execution of the laws, so far as this may be practicable, the Executive has no authority to decide what shall be the relations between the federal government and South Carolina. He has been invested with no such discretion. He possesses no power to change the relations heretofore existing between them, much less to acknowledge the independence of that State. This would be to invest a mere executive officer with the power of recognizing the dissolution of the confederacy among our thirty-three sovereign States. It bears no resemblance to the recognition of a foreign *de facto* government, involving no such responsibility. Any attempt to do this would, on his part, be a naked act of usurpation. It is, therefore, my duty to submit to Congress the whole question in all its bearings.'

"Such is my opinion still. I could therefore meet you only as private gentlemen of the highest character, and was entirely willing to communicate to Congress any proposition you might have to make to that body upon the subject. Of this you were well aware. It was my earnest desire that such a disposition might be made of the whole subject by Congress, who alone possess the power, as to prevent the inauguration of a civil war between the parties in regard to the possession of the federal forts in the harbor of Charleston, and I therefore deeply regret that, in your opinion, 'the events of the last twenty-four hours render this impossible.'"

The import of this language cannot well be mistaken. Its assertions are to the full effect of repudiating official relations between South Carolina as a foreign government and himself as President of the United States, and a reference of the whole question to Congress. It is addressed to Robert W. Barnwell, James H. Adams, and James L. Orr, "with great personal regard," and not to the commissioners who aspired to represent the sovereignty of an independent and foreign State. It is perhaps needless, though it may be well to notice, that the representatives of South Carolina, while admitting this attitude of the President towards them, fortified the dignity of their position with the subsequent written declaration that "they felt no special solicitude as to the character in which you (the President) might recognize us, (the commissioners.") If diplomatic relations suppose a mutuality of official character, it is quite certain that the personal appearance of James Buchanan, in this correspondence, deprives it of its imputed nature. The simplest mind will not have failed to perceive that so far from an official recognition by the President of the United States of the government of South Carolina having occurred, not only was its prudence but its possibility denied, and "the whole question" was referred to the arbitrament of Congress. Indeed, to such a reference by the President, in pursuance of the intent thus expressed, is it that the majority of the committee are now empowered to pervert his declarations and acts into evidences of a censurable correspondence with a rebellious State. It is conceded that the further effusion of words upon this topic of investigation would be an extravagant expenditure of both time and labor. The simplicity of the case can in nowise detract from its strength. Its perfect symmetry of proportion commends to the public that admirable prudence which preserved unsullied from even approximate reproach the purity of the presidential character when remitting to Congress the decision of a purely constitutional question.

But we are admonished by the majority of the committee that the presidential ermine was sullied in the epistolary correspondence which at a later date occurred between Hon. J. Holt, Secretary of War *ad interim*, on the part of the government, and Hon. I. W. Hayne, envoy from the State of South Carolina, bearing a communication from the governor of that State to the President of the United States in relation to the surrender of Fort Sumter. It must be remembered that the correspondence communicated to the House in no instance discloses either personal or epistolary intercourse between the President and the envoy. Senatorial intervention diverted the latter from the prosecution of his purpose, and substituted for his a communication from certain senators to the President upon the controverted questions. It may be well to reproduce at this point the communication referred to. It is as follows:

"SENATE CHAMBER, *January* 11, 1861.

"SIR: We have been requested to present to you copies of a correspondence between certain senators of the United States and Colonel Isaac W. Hayne, now in this city, in behalf of the government of South Carolina; and to ask that you will take into consideration the subject of said correspondence.

"Very respectfully, your obedient servants,

"BEN. FITZPATRICK.
"S. R. MALLORY.
"JOHN SLIDELL.

"His Excellency JAMES BUCHANAN,
"*President of the United States.*"

Proceeding through a constitutional channel, the subject of inquiry and demand thus unexceptionably submitted to his notice received from the President a fitting response through the Secretary of War *ad interim*. The following extract affirms the continued and careful scrupulousness with which the constitutional integrity of the chief executive officer was guarded and the dignity of the government maintained:

"In regard to the proposition of Colonel Hayne, 'that no re-enforcements will be sent to Fort Sumter in the interval, and that public peace will not be disturbed by any act of hostility towards South Carolina,' it is impossible for me to give you any such assurances. The President has no authority to enter into such an agreement or understanding. As an executive officer, he is simply bound to protect the public property, so far as this may be practicable; and it would be a manifest violation of his duty to place himself under engagements that he would not perform this duty either for an indefinite or a limited period. At the present moment, it is not deemed necessary to re-enforce Major Anderson, because he makes no such request, and feels quite secure in his position. Should his safety, however, require re-enforcements, every effort will be made to supply them.

"In regard to an assurance from the President 'that public peace will not be disturbed by any act of hostility towards South Carolina,' the answer will readily occur to yourselves. To Congress, and to Congress alone, belongs the power to make war, and it would be an act of usurpation for the Executive to give any assurance that Congress would not exercise this power, however strongly he may be convinced that no such intention exists."

It is not possible that a more successful refutation of the charge against the President of diplomatic intercourse with representatives accredited from the State of South Carolina could be either constructed or imagined. With characteristic care even the remotest advances to such a consummation were distinctively repelled. The most casual conversations were rescued from perversion by remarkable precautions, and the self-imposed restraint of South Carolina was the result rather of the influences of her citizens than of any assurances alledged to have been given by the Executive. In the whole course of the published correspondence it will be impossible to detect the most trifling deviation from the earliest annunciation by the President in his message to Congress at its opening, of his intention to defend with the whole power of the government its property, and to conserve its rights with all his constitutional vigor. The ardent inspirations of an uncalculating zeal have denounced as timidity these dictates of sobriety; impulsive impetuosity has derided them, and the ungenerous impulses of political hostility have visited upon them the invectives of acrimonious controversy. But the sober sense of the public will inevitably prevail over these factitious stimulants of factious discord. Ultimately will be recognized and acknowledged the prescient wisdom which palliated the shock of disunion by the preservation of peace, which preserved from desolation by barricading the paths of blood, and wooed the occasion for conciliation, compromise and adjustment by the counsels of moderation and peace. That the evening light still lingers in the parting day, and that to a people's prayers and hopes the night hath not yet come, may with truth be ascribed to the equable action of the President. It is to be regretted that the stridulous cry of partisan politics penetrates through and rises above the dismal moan of a dissolving republic. It is sad to think how reproaches exhaust the energies, and invectives occupy the faculties, that a less disordered temperament or a more equally poised intellect would have devoted to harmonious co-operation, and have crowned with national preservation. It is, however, to be entertained as one—not the least alarming—of the current expositions of the day; and the philosophic observer, however he be depressed by the reflection, will not probably err in his estimate of the hopelessness of our condition when including this among the signs and wonders of the latter days. I would not willingly encourage by defending the delinquency of any public officer. The more elevated his position, the greater should be the exactions upon his virtue and capacity. But the distressing proneness of the professional party critic to detract from official virtue, and the tendency of party spirit to defame political adversaries, should be indicated in their inception, and be transfixed with the public reprobation. I do not apply these reflections to the report of the majority of the committee, but I am clearly of opinion that their remembrance would disarm its perusal of some of its baneful effects.

JOHN COCHRANE.

I concur in the conclusions and in most of the views above expressed.

L. O'B. BRANCH.

www.ingramcontent.com/pod-product-compliance
Lightning Source LLC
LaVergne TN
LVHW020643110826
845149LV00004B/1329

9781418189570